MYSTERY FISH

SECRETS OF THE COELACANTH

BY SALLY M. WALKER
ILLUSTRATIONS BY SHAWN GOULD

On My Own
SCIENCE

M Millbrook Press/Minneapolis

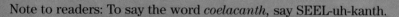

Note to readers: To say the word *coelacanth*, say SEEL-uh-kanth.

Text copyright © 2006 by Sally M. Walker
Illustrations copyright © 2006 by Shawn Gould

Millbrook Press
A division of Lerner Publishing Group
241 First Avenue North
Minneapolis, MN 55401 U.S.A.

Website address: www.lernerbooks.com

Library of Congress Cataloging-in-Publication Data

Walker, Sally M.
    Mystery fish : secrets of the coelacanth / by Sally M. Walker ; illustrations by Shawn Gould.
        p.   cm. — (On my own science)
    ISBN: 1–57505–638–0 (lib. bdg. : alk. paper)
    1. Coelacanth—Juvenile literature. I. Gould, Shawn, ill. II. Title. III. Series.
QL638.L26W364 2006
597.3'9—dc22   2004013865

Manufactured in the United States of America
1 2 3 4 5 6 – DP – 11 10 09 08 07 06

For Roslyn Emily Stobbs and her grandpa
Robin—have fun sharing fish tales
—S.M.W.

To my parents, Roger and Cindy Gould
—S.G.

A STRANGE BLUE FISH
South Africa, 1938

What a strange blue fish!
Marjorie Courtenay-Latimer stood
on the fishing boat and stared.
She had seen many kinds of fish.
She collected them for the museum
where she worked.
But she had never seen a fish like this one.
It was almost as big as a person.
It had four thick fins
that looked like stubby legs.
The fish's scales had pointy spines.
Its tail had a funny-looking tip.

This fish was a real mystery.

Marjorie took it to the museum.

She looked at the pictures
in her fish books.

None looked like the big, blue fish.

Marjorie started to worry.

The weather was quite warm.

The fish's body might rot in the hot air.

Then no one would be able to study it.

Marjorie needed to cool the fish
to keep it from rotting.

Only two refrigerators in her town
were big enough to hold it.

Their owners said no.

What would happen to the mystery fish?

Marjorie sent a drawing of the fish
to an expert named J. L. B. Smith.
Maybe he would know what it was.
Days passed.
The fish's body turned dark brown.
It started to rot.
Finally, only the skin could be saved.
Marjorie had the skin stuffed.

Marjorie's drawing stunned
J. L. B. Smith.
It looked like a kind of fish
that had lived long, long ago.
Fish of this kind are called coelacanths.
They lived during the time of the
dinosaurs, millions of years ago.

Scientists had found coelacanth fossils.
But no scientist had ever
seen a live coelacanth.
Everyone believed that these fish had
died out when the dinosaurs did.
Yet Marjorie's fish had been
caught alive, just weeks before.
Could it be a coelacanth?

To find out, Smith
went to see the fish.
He could hardly believe his eyes.
It really was a coelacanth!
The body had rotted.
But he could study the skin and fins.
He saw that the fins were thick and rounded.

Fins with this shape are called lobed fins.

Few other living fish have them.

How did the fins work?

Did the coelacanth use them to walk

on the bottom of the ocean?

And how did the fish

use its strangely shaped tail?

Smith searched for years
for another coelacanth to study.
At last, a fisher caught one in 1952,
in the Comoro Islands.
These small islands are east of Africa.
Smith cut open the fish's
body and studied its parts.
He learned many things about
how a coelacanth's body works.
But he couldn't answer his questions
about the fins and tail.
Other scientists also studied dead
coelacanths that fishers caught.
They asked many questions.
Do coelacanths live in deep water?
How do they hunt for food?
To solve these mysteries, someone would have
to find the fish in their underwater home.

BENEATH THE WAVES
Comoro Islands, January 1987

Hans Fricke's mini submarine
cruised deep underwater.
Hans was a scientist from Germany.
He had come to the Comoro Islands
to search for coelacanths.
He wanted to find their habitat,
the place where they lived.
The mini submarine was called *Geo*.
Only two people could fit in it.
But they could search underwater much
longer than swimmers or divers could.
Geo had a spotlight to light the dark water.
Its camera could make underwater movies.
And its metal arm could pick up
objects from the ocean bottom.

Hans and his friend Jürgen Schauer
piloted *Geo* along a steep underwater cliff.
They could see the openings of dark caves.
But they didn't look inside.
Hans thought that coelacanths were
too big to live inside a cave.
He and Jürgen saw lots of fish,
but no coelacanths.
Where could they be?
Hans needed more clues
to find these mystery fish.
He talked with Comoran fishers.
They told him that coelacanths
had been caught only at night.
And they suggested places to look.

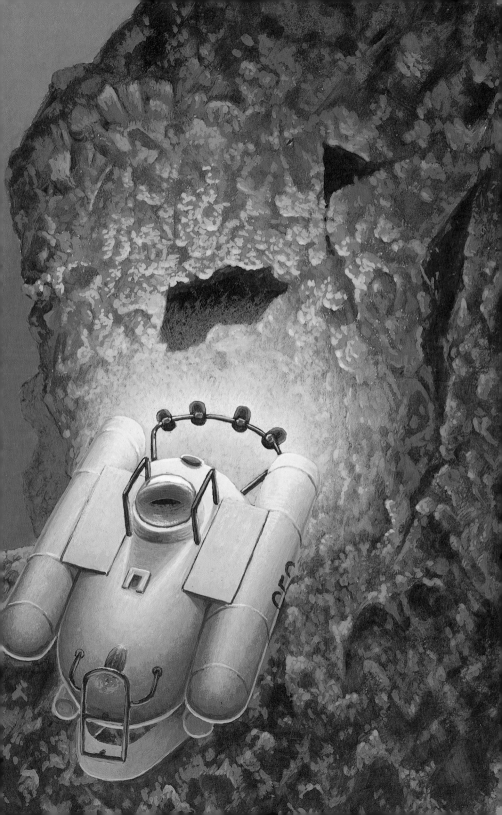

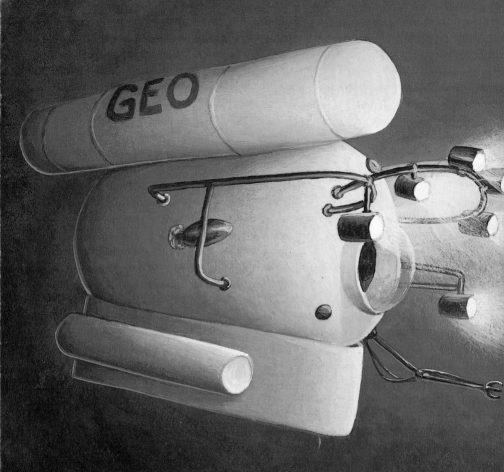

The crew started diving at night.
Geo cruised through inky black water.
Its spotlights made bright
white circles in the darkness.
Weeks passed.
The crew didn't find any coelacanths.

Hans had to go home to Germany
for an important meeting.
Jürgen and the other crew
members stayed behind.
They had just five more days
to find a coelacanth.
Then their money would run out.

That night, Jürgen piloted *Geo*
around some rocks.
At the edge of the light,
he saw two glowing circles.
Fish eyes!
Then Jürgen saw a rounded blue fin.

Finally, a coelacanth!
Jürgen and his helper
watched the coelacanth
for 20 minutes.
To swim, it paddled gracefully
with its lobed fins.

Then the fish did something strange.
Its tail tilted upward.
The fish moved into a headstand!
Jürgen had no idea why.
He took as many pictures as he could.
At last, the coelacanth swam away.

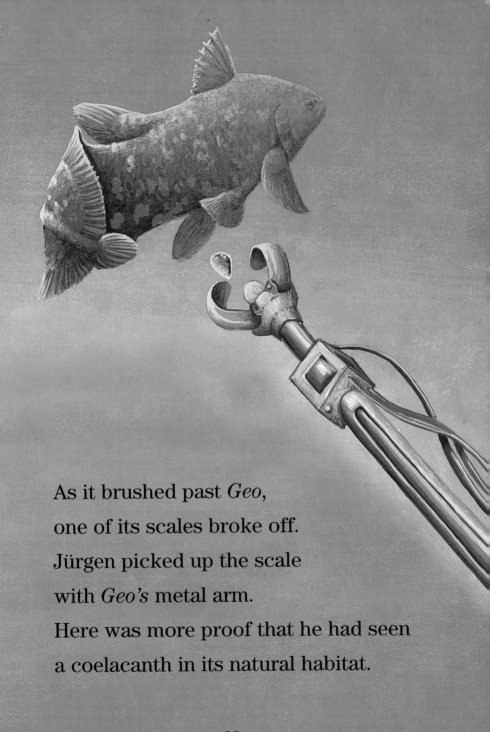

As it brushed past *Geo*,
one of its scales broke off.
Jürgen picked up the scale
with *Geo's* metal arm.
Here was more proof that he had seen
a coelacanth in its natural habitat.

FOLLOWING THE MYSTERY FISH
Comoro Islands, April 1987

A few months later, the crew
returned to the Comoro Islands.
They dove again in *Geo*.
Hans finally saw a coelacanth himself.
The crew filmed several of the fish.
None of the coelacanths
walked on its lobed fins.
J. L. B. Smith's idea had been wrong.

Geo's crew noticed that white spots
dotted each coelacanth's body.
Each fish had different spots.
A careful watcher could study
the spots to tell the fish apart.
The crew also saw that coelacanths
swim slowly.

Mostly they let the water
carry them along.
When a coelacanth swims,
its tiny tail tip bends from side to side.
The tail steers the fish around rocks.
It also helps the fish do headstands.

Hans wondered about those headstands.
What made a coelacanth do them?
He knew that *Geo* gave off a
small amount of electricity.
Maybe this electricity bothered coelacanths.
He made up a test to find out.
Hans put two metal posts on *Geo's* arm.

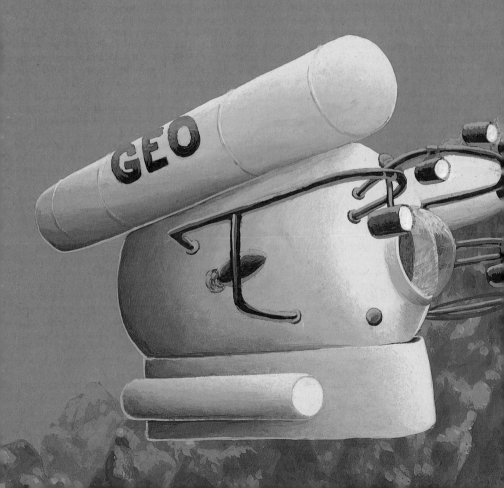

Each post could send
electricity into the water.
The crew steered *Geo* toward
two coelacanths.
Hans used *Geo's* arm to point
the posts at the fish.
Both fish did headstands!
Hans had solved another puzzle.

One morning, the crew explored
a steep underwater cliff.
They were inside *Jago*,
a new mini submarine.
Jago's spotlights shone into a cave.
Bright circles glowed inside.
Coelacanth eyes!
Another mystery was solved.
Coelacanths stay in caves during the day.
Caves are good hiding places.

They protect coelacanths
from predators, animals that
kill other animals for food.
Caves are also good resting places.
The walls protect fish from the flow
of water outside the cave.
Moving water can sweep fish away
unless they swim against it.
In a cave, fish can rest
safely without swimming.

Hans had learned that
coelacanths rest during the day
and swim at night.
He thought they probably hunted
during their nightly swims.
Where did they go?
No one had ever seen a
coelacanth catch its food.
But the stomachs of dead
coelacanths contained fish that
live in deep water.
Hans guessed that
coelacanths hunted in deep
water at night.
How could he prove it?
Jürgen helped solve this mystery.

He made special tags
and stuck each tag onto a dart.
Then he placed a dart gun
on the outside of *Jago*.

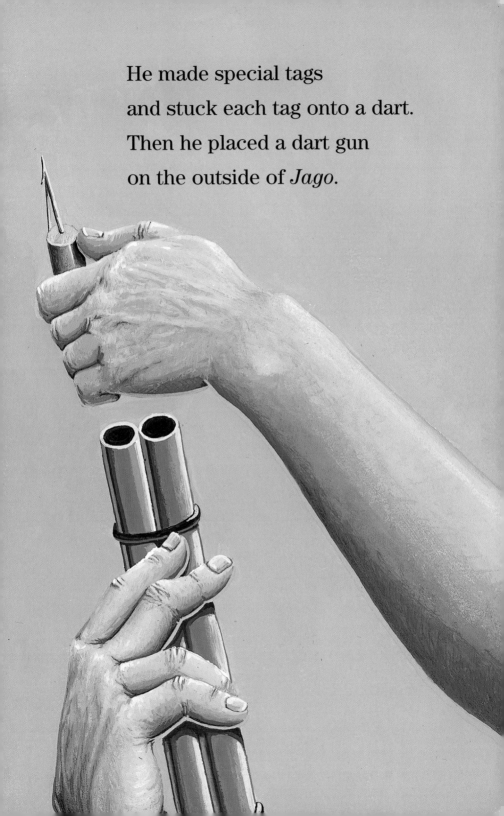

The crew used the gun to shoot the darts
into the scales of 11 coelacanths.
The darts didn't hurt the coelacanths.
They just held the tags in place.
Each tag sent signals through the water
to a boat on the surface.
The signals told Hans where
the coelacanths went.

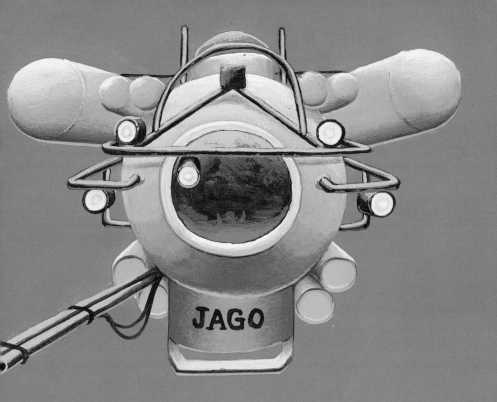

Each evening, they swam from their caves.
Hunting alone, they slowly
moved down into deep water
and then up again.
As the sun came up, the fish
swam to the nearest cave.
Safe inside, they rested
until their next hunt.

THE SEARCH CONTINUES
Indonesia, 1997

Fish expert Mark Erdmann

gazed at the animal on the cart.

It had lobed fins and a tip on its tail.

This fish had to be a coelacanth.

Mark knew that coelacanths lived

near the Comoro Islands.

But he was in a fish market

6,000 miles away, in Indonesia!

Was it possible that coelacanths

lived here?

Mark and his wife, Arnaz,

asked fishers to help them find out.

In July 1998, a fisher came
to the Erdmanns' house.
He had caught a coelacanth.
It was still alive!
Mark and Arnaz climbed into
the water with the fish.
They tried to keep it alive.
Sadly, it soon died.

Mark studied the fish's body.

It was different from other coelacanths.

Its scales were gold instead of blue.

Mark did many tests.

He learned that the fish was a

new kind of coelacanth!

The next coelacanth surprise
came in South Africa.
It was October 2000.
Pieter Venter and two friends
were scuba diving in deep water.
Pieter was shocked to see a coelacanth
swimming near a rocky ledge.

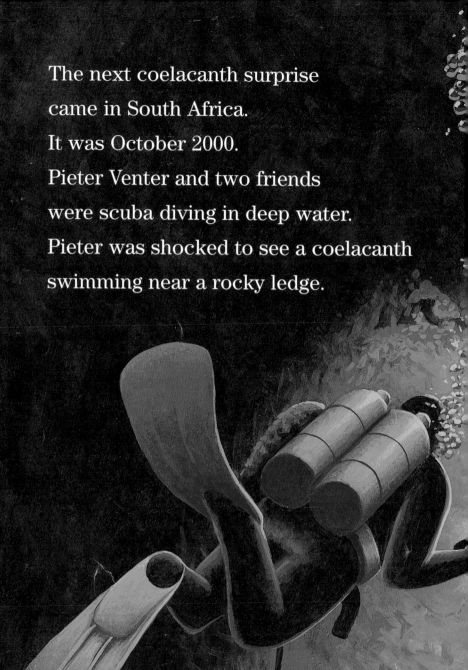

No coelacanths had been found
in South Africa since Marjorie's fish.
On later dives, Pieter and his friends
saw more coelacanths.
And *Jago's* crew saw 15 when they
dove in South Africa in 2002.

Coelacanths live in more places
than people once thought.
But no one knows for sure how many
coelacanths live around the world.
Most experts believe that
there are only a few hundred.
If too many of those fish are caught,
coelacanths could die out forever.
People are working to make sure
that this won't happen.
It's against the law to catch
or kill coelacanths anywhere.
Some countries have created underwater
parks where people cannot go.
These parks are safe places for all fish.

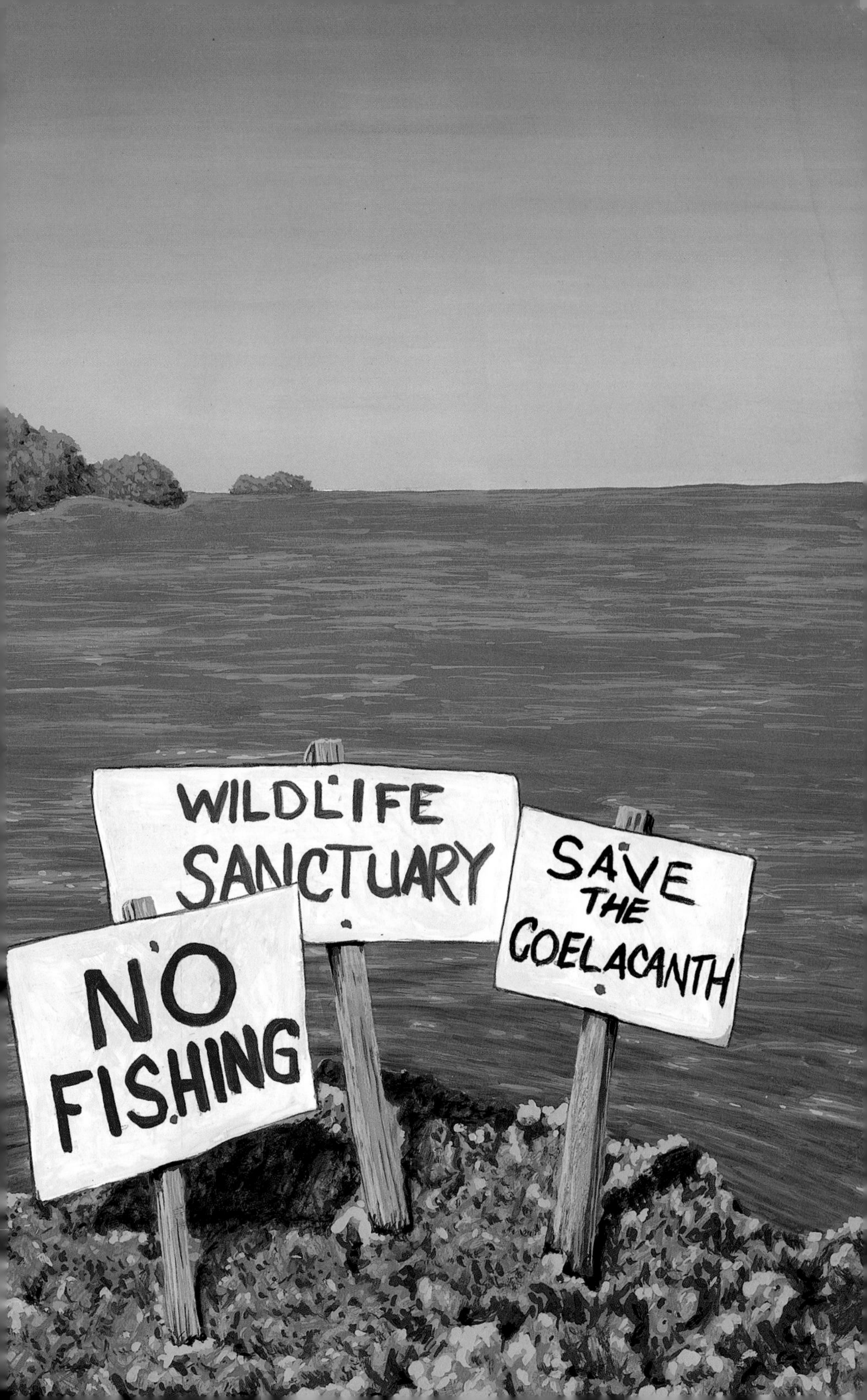
WILDLIFE SANCTUARY
SAVE THE COELACANTH
NO FISHING

Many coelacanth mysteries remain.
Do the fish have homes we
haven't yet found?
How do they catch food?
The biggest puzzle is about
baby coelacanths, or pups.
No scientist has ever seen a living pup.

Where do pups live?

How do they grow?

All over the world, scientists
are asking questions like these.
Maybe the answers will lead us to other
exciting coelacanth mysteries.

TIMELINE

1938—Marjorie Courtenay-Latimer found a strange blue fish on a fishing boat.

1939—J. L. B. Smith said the fish was a coelacanth. He gave it the scientific name *Latimeria chalumnae*.

1952—A fisher in the Comoro Islands caught another coelacanth.

1987—In the Comoro Islands, Hans Fricke and his team searched for coelacanths in a mini submarine called *Geo*. Jürgen Schauer saw a live coelacanth.

1989—Hans Fricke and his team found coelacanths living in caves.

1997—Mark Erdmann saw a coelacanth in a fish market in the Asian country of Indonesia.

1998—A fisher brought a coelacanth to Mark Erdmann. He and his wife swam with the fish and studied it after it died.

1999—Mark Erdmann learned that his coelacanth was a new kind.

2000—Pieter Venter and his diving team found coelacanths in Sodwana Bay, South Africa.

2001—Pieter Venter and his team found the largest coelacanth ever. It was more than 6.5 feet long.

2004—Four coelacanths were caught off the coast of Tanzania, Africa.

GLOSSARY

fins: body parts that fish use to swim and steer

habitat: the place where an animal normally lives and grows

lobed fins: rounded, fleshy fins. Most fish fins are flat.

predators: animals that kill other animals for food

pups: baby coelacanths

scales: flat, hard plates that cover and protect the bodies of most kinds of fish

Courtena
 Disco
 Crypt
Erdmann   to
 Scient   *ishes*
 54 (19
Erdmann
 Natur
Forey, Pe
 Chapn
Fricke, H
 Time
 (June
Fricke, H   and
 Body
 Fishes
Smith, J.
 Trans
Smith, J.
 Longn
Thomson
 York:
Walker, S   h.
 Minne
Weinberg
 Coela